IELTS GENERAL WRITING

How To Write 8+ Answers For The IELTS Exam!

(With High Scoring Sample Answers For Each Question Type)

By Daniella Moyla

IELTS General Writing

How To Write 8+ Answers For The IELTS Exam!

Copyright 2017 by Daniella Moyla

Published by Sanbrook Publishing

ISBN-13: 978-1542843805

All rights reserved. No Part of this book may be reproduced or transmitted in any form or by any means without the written permission of the author.

Limits of Liability / Disclaimer of Warranty:

The author and publisher of this book and the accompanying materials have used their best efforts in preparing this program. The author and publisher make no representation or warranties with respect to the accuracy, applicability, fitness, or completeness of the contents of this book. They disclaim any warranties (expressed or implied), merchantability, or fitness for any particular purpose. The author and publisher shall in no event be held liable for any loss or other damage, including but not limited to special, incidental, consequential, or other damages.

This manual contains material protected under International and Federal Copyright Laws and Treaties. Any unauthorized reprint or use of this material is prohibited.

IELTS is jointly owned by British Council, IDP: IELTS Australia and the University of Cambridge ESOL Examinations (Cambridge ESOL).

*****

Table of Contents

WHO IS THIS BOOK FOR? 1
GENERAL TRAINING WRITING SECTION 3
TASK 1 WRITING GENERAL TRAINING 5
    What Is Task 1? 5
    Suggested Answer Structure (Task 1) 5
    Scoring Criteria (Task 1) 6
    Task 1 Question Types 7
        Formal 7
        Semi-formal 8
        Informal 9
    Planning Task 1 Letters 9
    Quick Tips For Task 1 11
HIGH SCORING TASK 1 SAMPLE LETTERS 14
    Formal – Sample 1 14
    Formal – Sample 2 16
    Semi-formal – Sample 1 18
    Semi-formal – Sample 2 20
    Informal – Sample 1 22
    Informal – Sample 2 24
TASK 2 WRITING ACADEMIC 27
    What Is Task 2? 27
    Suggested Answer Structure (Task 2) 27
    Scoring Criteria (Task 2) 29
    Task 2 Question Types 30
        Opposing-Views Question (formerly known as Argument) 30
        Opinion-Based Question (formerly known as Proposal) 31
        Two-Part Question (formerly known as Discussion) 34
    Task 2 Question Types Summary 36
    Task 2 Question Types (Mind Map) 37

- Planning Task 2 Essays 38
- Quick Tips For Task 2 42

HIGH SCORING TASK 2 SAMPLE ANSWERS 45
- Opposing-Views Question Type 45
- Opinion-based Question Type 53
- Two-part Question Type 65

ABOUT THE AUTHOR 74

WHO IS THIS BOOK FOR?

The IELTS (General Training) can be a very daunting exam in which to achieve a high score. The significance of the IELTS can be the difference between obtaining a visa or position at a university for many people.

Therefore, it is important that if you require an IELTS score of 8 or above, you review what makes high quality writing answers before you take the exam.

All too many people take the IELTS several times without reaching their desired score and do not understand why.

This book has been written specifically for people like you who want to view sample writing answers that comply with the standards of the IELTS scoring criteria and would achieve a high score if written for an IELTS exam.

Many sample answers on the internet today are not quality reviewed and can be misleading.

The answers you will find in this book, however, have been written by a professional IELTS teacher with more than 10 years experience who has used these methods to reach high scoring results with most of her students.

If you want to succeed on the IELTS Writing section, then this book will assist you in understanding what is required.

You should read this book if:

- You have taken the IELTS exam before and did not obtain a high score in the writing section and don't know why.

- You have searched the internet for sample answers but you are unsure of the quality of the answers and who wrote them.

- You have never taken the IELTS exam and you want to review how high scoring answers are structured, so you can follow a similar format.

- Your IELTS exam is very soon and you need last minute guidance on how to write high scoring answers.

GENERAL TRAINING WRITING SECTION

The Writing section of the IELTS has two formats, Academic and General Training.

This book refers to the **General Training format**, which is often one of the main requirements for candidates interested in obtaining a visa or job in most English speaking countries.

The writing section assesses a person's ability to communicate in written English, in an academic context as well as the capacity to understand different tasks and respond to them with an adequate level of accuracy.

	Writing Section	
Task	One: Letter	Two: Essay
Duration	20 minutes	40 minutes
Word Count	150 words	250 words
Description	Candidates are presented with a situation to which they have to respond in a letter format.	Candidates are given a question which needs to be answered in an essay format.

Even though there is an allocation of time for each task, candidates are responsible for managing their own time, as one hour is given to complete the whole writing section. Which means, that if a candidate spends more than twenty minutes in task 1, this will reduce their time to write the essay which will be detrimental for the final result.

It is also important to remember that task 2 (the essay) is worth double the marks, and therefore requires more attention given its level of complexity.

TASK 1 WRITING GENERAL TRAINING

What Is Task 1?

This task in particular, evaluates a candidate's ability to communicate in a written manner understanding the cultural implications of the English Language. Candidates are expected to identify the purpose of a letter as well as the tone and register they should use in the missive.

The types of letter as well as level of formality will vary, and only one will be given per test. These can include the following:

a) Formal

b) Semi-formal

c) Informal

Suggested Answer Structure (Task 1)

The structure for the report may differ according to the type of situation received. Generally speaking, the letter will be divided in five sections including three main paragraphs.

Letter Structure	
Opening/salutation	The approach to address the recipient depends on the level of formality: • **Formal:** *"Dear Sir or Madam,"* • **Semi-formal:** *"Dear Mr/Mrs (Last name)"* • **Informal:** *"Dear (first name)"*

Introduction	The first paragraph needs to clearly state the purpose of the letter, for example: *"I am writing to complain about the way my case was handled"* Another factor to consider is introducing yourself. This may or may not be a bullet point from the question, but it is important to remember that in many situations the addressee of the letter might not know who the sender is. As a rule of thumb, all *formal* and most *semi-formal* letters request the writer to introduce him/herself.
Detailed Paragraph	This paragraph should directly answer the bullet points provided in the question and create a clear and believable context to the letter. This may be divided into more paragraphs if the topics in discussion vary from each other. There is no maximum of paragraphs in this type of task.
Closing paragraph	This paragraph should present the action the sender expects the recipient to take in regards to the letter.
Sign-off	The format to end the letter also depends on the level of formality: - **Formal:** *"Yours sincerely"* - **Semi-formal:** *"Yours faithfully"* - **Informal:** *"Best wishes"* The sign-off needs to match the opening.

Scoring Criteria (Task 1)

Task 1 is assessed according to four areas which determine the final score in bands from 1 to 9. A brief description of each criterion is provided below:

Scoring Criteria Task 1	
Task achievement	This criterion assesses how well the candidate responds to the situation given, proving enough details and using appropriate tone and register (the intention of the letter and the level of formality)
Cohesion and Coherence	This criterion assesses how well ideas are sequenced, connected, and organized.
Lexical resource	This criterion assesses the variety of vocabulary and level of sophistication used.
Grammatical range and accuracy	This criterion assesses the variety of structures used and how well they are used in terms of the frequency of errors.

*The public version of the Writing scoring criteria is available on www.ielts.org

Task 1 Question Types

A variety of situations can be included in this part of the writing section, however, only one is given per test. As mentioned above, the context of the letter as well as the level of formality will vary, including letters of apology, request, and complaint, among others. The level of formality will depend on the relationship the sender has with the recipient of the missive.

Formal

This type includes complaints and letters to agencies or other institutions, such as governmental. Another way to identify this type is when the context implies that there has been no previous communication between the writer and the receiver and therefore the relationship must be formal.

Example:

You have bought a new mobile phone and after a few days of purchase you discover a major flaw.
Write a letter to the company. In your letter...
- *Introduce yourself*
- *Explain the situation*
- *Say what action you would like to company to take.*

Semi-formal

This type includes all situations where the writer and receiver have been in contact before, but there is a formal relationship. For example, student to teacher, tenant to landlord and so on.

Example:

You have been offered a new position in the company you currently work for but the new role is in a foreign country. You want to take the job but your family commitments would not allow you to move abroad at the moment.
Write a letter to your supervisor. In your letter...
- *Thank for the new job offer*
- *Decline the job offer*
- *Recommend a colleague who might be suitable for the position.*

Informal

This case applies to all situations where the writer and receiver have a close relationship and therefore refer to each other by the first name. For example, friend to friend, relative to relative, classmate to classmate.

Example:

You are currently living abroad and want to share you experience with one of your best friends back home.
Write a letter to your friend. In your letter...
- *Describe your present life*
- *Tell him/her why you chose this country*
- *Invite him/her to come and visit you*

Planning Task 1 Letters

One of the main reasons people fail to get a high score in task 1, is due to the lack of context. Most people simplify their response to answering the bullet points given in the question without providing enough details that may not be explicitly part of the question. This is often the result of poor analysis and planning of the letter.

Therefore, it is vital to have a system to follow for task 1 that delivers better results.

Steps to follow:

Step 1 - Study the situation carefully

Read the question a couple of times to make sure you accurately identify the situation and the level of formality you should use.

Then study the bullet points carefully and decide if you need to add any more information to each point. The best way to plan for a letter is to think: *What would I do in that case?*

The more realistic the letter sounds, the better score you will receive.

Step 2 - Make a list of ideas to include in the letter

Use the page where the question is to make a short list of the aspects that will be part of the description. By doing this, you will avoid leaving information out and better present the purpose of the letter as well as the description of the situation.

Step 3 - Write the letter for the reader and not for you

This sounds rather obvious, but a common mistake people make in this task, is to take for granted certain information that is necessary even if it has not been mentioned in the question itself or bullet points. A good example of this is when candidates end the letter with a phrase such as: *"I look forward to hearing from you"* but forget to provide contact details. Another common case is when there is no information as to who is writing the letter. For instance:

"Dear Mr Smith,

I'm writing to request information about the project that will take place in our building next month."

In this situation, there is no reference about the writer, is the person writing a tenant of the building or an employee? This is why the writer needs to provide all information necessary

for the receiver to fully understand who is writing, what for and what is expected from him/her.

Step 4 - Check and edit your letter

Always leave a few minutes at the end to read your letter and make any changes necessary before you submit it. Most people understand this is important but usually run out of time before they get a chance to do it. The reality is, you should always have some minutes to spare. If you do not, that means you need more practice.

Quick Tips For Task 1

1) Have a system and manage your time wisely.

As explained above, most people do not have a system for any of the writing tasks. The reality is, most people are not used to the idea of planning at all and they think of it as a waste of time.

However, planning is vital in order to get good results. There is no perfect method for planning, but a good place to start is to follow the suggestions above.

Twenty minutes seems to be insufficient for planning, writing and checking. But again, having a system will help you get there. Keep track of how long it takes you to analyse a letter task, take notes and write.

Use that to create your own system and then practice as much as possible keeping records of the time you spend on each step. After a few trials you will see amazing results.

2) Get familiar with the scoring criteria

Understanding what examiners expect to see is essential. Even though the band descriptors are available on the IELTS official website, not many people have taken the time to try to understand what they actually are and how examiners use them.

But if you do not know what getting an 8 means, then how will you ever get there?

This is not rocket science. The descriptors are quite clear and though they might sound somewhat technical at times, even knowing the main aim of each criterion will help you recognize what examiners need to see in order to score you handsomely.

For example, in order to get a 7, you need to at least:

Task achievement

- Write at least 150 words and submit a finished letter

- Present a clear purpose to the letter

- Address every bullet point and add any necessary details that will help the development, though some could be better covered

Cohesion and Coherence

- Present the information in a logical sequence where ideas progress at ease

- Use a range of cohesive devices (linking words, pronoun reference etc.) with some flexibility though there may be some under/over-use

Lexical range and accuracy

- Use a variety of expressions with some level of sophistication (uncommon words) and some awareness of style and collocation.

- Have a few errors throughout (most sentences are error-free) in terms of spelling, word choice and form.

Grammatical range and accuracy

- Have a variety of structures with a high level of accuracy (most sentences are error-free) and there is good control over punctuation.

As it can be seen, a letter that gets a 7 is far from being perfect, but it needs to have a high level of accuracy in all four criteria.

In order to get 8, the requirements are the same but there is less room for error and higher expectations in terms of the proficiency in the use of vocabulary and grammar.

HIGH SCORING TASK 1 SAMPLE LETTERS

Formal – Sample 1

Question:

> You are a student at a prestigious university about to graduate. You have been offered to continue studying a Masters program with a scholarship for your academic merits. However, you have been offered a job at big firm and have already accepted it.
>
> Write a letter to the Dean. In your letter...
> - Thank the university for the offer
> - Decline the offer
> - Find out if you are able to accept the scholarship in the future

Planning:

The letter is: formal because it is addressed to a high authority

The purpose is to: thank/decline a study offer

Sender: Student

Receiver: Dean

> You are a student at a prestigious university about to graduate. You have been offered to continue studying a Masters program with a scholarship for your academic merits. However, you have been offered a job at big firm and have already accepted it.
>
> Write a letter to the Dean. In your letter...
> - Thank the university for the offer → I feel honoured/did not expect/very thankful
> - Decline the offer → Unfortunately I am unable/XX company hired me
> - Find out if you are able to accept the scholarship in the future → Is it possible to accept this offer for next year?

Sample Answer 1:

Dear Dean Rickard

My name is John Smith, current student of this university. I am close to graduating from the Psychology program and have been given the award of Excellence for my academic achievements. To my huge surprise, I have also been offered a position in the Masters program of Psychology and granted a scholarship that covers all fees by this respected institution. The purpose of my letter is respectfully decline this generous offer.

Let me start by showing my most heart-felt appreciation for considering me for this incredible opportunity. I feel extremely honoured and terribly sorry for having to decline such offer. The reason being, a job I was offered just a couple of weeks ago in one of the biggest Counselling Clinics of the country which will allow me to get experience in the field I studied.

I have explained the situation to my new employer and they offered me to do the Masters part-time from next year onwards. Would it be possible for me to deter the offer till next year?

If this is not possible, I completely understand and would like to once again express my gratitude for extending this one of a kind opportunity to me.

Yours sincerely,

John Smith

(205 words)

Formal – Sample 2

Question:

> You bought a book online as a present for your father on his birthday. You ordered the book a month in advance as the website stated delivery would take 10 business days. It's been more than 15 business days now and you still haven't received the book.
>
> Write a letter to the company. In your letter…
>
> - Explain the situation
> - Complain about the inconvenience
> - Describe what actions you want the company to take

Planning:

The letter is: formal because it is a complaint

The purpose is to: explain/complain and request

Sender: Customer

Receiver: Company

> (You bought) a book online as a present for your father on his birthday. You ordered the book a month in advance as the website stated delivery would take 10 business days. It's been more than 15 business days now and you still haven't received the book.
>
> Write a letter (to the company.) In your letter…
>
> - Explain the situation ⟶ *Frequent customer/bought book 15 bd ago*
> - Complain about the inconvenience ⟶ *Book not delivered yet/make other arrangements*
> - Describe what actions you want the company to take ⟶ *Give date of arrival/or cancel purchase*

Sample Answer 2:

Dear Sir or Madam,

I am a frequent customer of your online shop and have always been quite satisfied with your service. However, in this occasion I am writing to complain about the following situation.

A month ago, I purchased the book "Parenting with NLP" as a present for my father whose birthday is in just few days. When I placed the order, the site advised that the book would be shipped the next day and that delivery should take between 8 to 10 business days.

The reason for my complaint is that it has been over 15 working days and the book still has not been delivered which puts me in a difficult situation as I will have to make other arrangements for my father's present.

I have never experienced such delays when using your service and this is probably the worst time to be having such issues. I would like to know how certain you are that the book will be here in time for my father's birthday. If I cannot receive a guarantee of this, I would like to cancel the order as I will have to purchase a different product.

I look forward to hearing from you. My mobile number as well as email address are provided in my business card enclosed in this letter.

Yours faithfully,

Tim Jones

(217 words)

Semi-formal – Sample 1

Question:

> You live in rented accommodation. One evening while preparing dinner, one of the kitchen appliances suddenly broke down.
>
> Write a letter to your landlord. In your letter...
> - Explain the situation
> - Apologize for the accident
> - Find out who is responsible for the repairing

Planning:

<u>The letter is:</u> semi-formal because you have been in contact with your landlord before

<u>The purpose is to:</u> explain/apologize and request information

<u>Sender</u>: Tenant

<u>Receiver</u>: Landlord

(You live in rented accommodation.) One evening while preparing dinner, one of the kitchen appliances suddenly broke down.

Write a letter to (your landlord.) In your letter...

- <u>Explain</u> the situation → *Was cooking/loud noise and smoke from oven*
- <u>Apologize</u> for the accident → *Very sorry/never had a problem like this before*
- <u>Find out</u> who is responsible for the repairing → *Does insurance cover?/we can split the cost/please send someone this week*

Sample Answer 1:

Dear Mr Young,

My name is Lisa, I'm the tenant of Unit 2/34 Vernon Rd, in Riversdale. I'm writing this letter to inform you about a rather unpleasant situation that occurred last night.

At about 7pm last night, I was preparing myself some dinner when all of a sudden I heard a loud noise coming from the oven. I turned around to see what it was and saw smoke coming out of it. I was a bit scared to open it and when I did, I couldn't find anything that could have caused the explosion. I was using the oven at the time, but I had never had any problems with this appliance before. When I tried to turn the oven on again, it wasn't working anymore.

I'm very sorry about this situation. I'm honestly not sure what could have caused the problem. I would like to find a solution as soon as possible because I do use the oven quite a bit.

Do you know if this is covered by the home insurance? If not, I am happy to split the cost of the repair. Please let me know if you can arrange for someone to come and fix it during this week if possible.

I look forward to hearing from you. My mobile number hasn't changed.

Yours sincerely,

Lisa Adams

(217 words)

Semi-formal – Sample 2

Question:

> You are planning to study a course but need to request a loan in order to enrol because you do not have enough funds.
>
> Write a letter to your bank agent. In your letter...
> - Explain the reason for the loan request
> - Find out what options the bank can offer you
> - Propose a method of paying back the loan

Planning:

<u>The letter is:</u> semi- formal because you have been in contact with your bank agent before

<u>The purpose is to:</u> explain/ request information/propose

<u>Sender</u>: Customer

<u>Receiver</u>: Bank agent

> You are planning to study a (course) but need to request a loan in order to enrol because you do not have enough funds.
>
> Write a letter to (your bank agent). In your letter...
> - <u>Explain</u> the reason for the loan request → Masters degree/need $15k / have $5k in savings
> - <u>Find out</u> what options the bank can offer you → Have no debt/do I qualify?/types of loans and interests?
> - <u>Propose</u> a method of paying back the loan → Full-time job/repay in 3 years monthly instalments

Sample Answer 2:

Dear Mrs Lee,

My name is Peter Jackson, I have been a customer of this bank for 5 years now. On this occasion I am writing to request a personal loan of $15.000.

The reason for my request is that I would like to study a Masters degree in the area of Finance. This is because I realize that in this competitive market, having just one degree does not seem to be enough to keep progressing in my career. However, I do not have the sum I need to enrol in the program. My savings only account to $5000 but the total fees are $20.000.

For this reason, I would like to know if having no other debts with the bank as well as my current income, would qualify for this personal loan. If that was the case, I would welcome information about the types of loans available at the moment as well as the interest rates I would be charged. As a full-time employee, I estimate I would be able to pay off the loan in 3 years, with monthly instalments.

Please let me know if this is possible so I otherwise make other arrangements or find other banks that might be able to assist me.

Yours sincerely,

Peter Jackson

(206 words)

Informal – Sample 1

Question:

> Your best friend has sent you an invitation to his/her wedding but being new to your workplace you are unable to take time off to attend.
>
> Write a letter to your friend. In your letter...
>
> - **Explain the situation**
> - **Apologize for not being able to go**
> - **Offer to visit sometime in the future**

Planning:

The letter is: in formal because you are writing to a person you have a close relationship with

The purpose is to: explain/ apologize/offer

Sender: Friend

Receiver: Friend

> (Your best friend) has sent you an invitation to his/her wedding but being new to your workplace you are unable to take time off to attend.
>
> Write a letter (to your friend). In your letter...
>
> - Explain the situation → Started job 2 months ago/Not enough leave/can't go
> - Apologize for not being able to go → So sorry/sent a present/asked Lisa to skype
> - Offer to visit sometime in the future → Will go to visit in July/we can catch up

Sample Answer 1:

Dear Anna,

I hope this letter finds you well. I was so excited to receive your wedding invitation. I'm so happy for you and Rob, you two make the perfect couple. Unfortunately, I'm writing to let you know I won't be able to make it to your special day.

The reason is, as you know, I've only started this job two months ago, which means I haven't accrued enough leave. I would need at least a week to make the trip back home and this is the busiest time in our office. I already asked my supervisor and he told me that the company only considers giving early leave to employees who have worked here for at least 6 months.

I can't begin to explain how sorry I am that I will miss seeing you walk down the aisle with your husband to be. I have, although, sent a present and hope it gets there in time before the wedding. I've also asked Lisa to connect to skype during the ceremony so I can still see you from home.

Moreover, I've already made plans to go there in July so we will have plenty of time to catch up. I want to see all the photos!

All the best,

Alex

(207 words)

Informal – Sample 2

Question:

> You work for an international company. You have been preparing for an important client meeting for months and suddenly find out that your mother has fallen severely ill and are requested by your family to travel to visit your mother.
>
> Write a letter to your colleague. In your letter...
>
> - Thank your colleague for helping you
> - Request your colleague to conduct the meeting on your behalf
> - Describe the details your colleague needs to know about the meeting

Planning:

The letter is: in formal because you are writing to a person you see on a daily basis

The purpose is to: thank/ request/describe

Sender: Colleague

Receiver: Colleague

You work for an international company. You have been preparing for an important client meeting for months and suddenly find out that your mother has fallen severely ill and are requested by your family to travel to visit your mother.

Write a letter to your colleague. In your letter...

- Thank your colleague for helping you → *Thanks for your support*
- Request your colleague to conduct the meeting on your behalf → *McDowell meeting/next Tuesday*
- Describe the details your colleague needs to know about the meeting → *Close deal/all details are ready /confirm with client/book room/study key points*

Sample Answer 2:

Dear Julia,

Thank you so much for offering to help me in this difficult time for me and my family. If the situation wasn't this serious, I wouldn't be taking leave at such busy time at work.

As you know, my mother is seriously ill and doctors haven't given a very positive diagnosis. For this reason I've been asked by my relatives to visit my mum just in case her situation worsens.

I have a few projects on my plate at the moment, but the most urgent is the McDowell meeting which is scheduled for next Tuesday. Since I won't be here next week, I was hoping you could conduct the meeting for me.

The purpose of this meeting is to close the deal and get the contract signed. The presentations is just an update of what has been offered. So I'll leave the folder with copies of the contract for all participants as well as the PPT which is now ready to go. All you have to do at this point is to confirm the meeting the client, book the meeting room and get familiarized with the key points of discussion.

Thanks again for being so kind and offering your support. Please don't hesitate to contact me at any time. You have my email address and mobile number.

Best regards,

Tony

(219 words)

TASK 2 WRITING ACADEMIC

What Is Task 2?

Task 2 consists of a question about general knowledge that needs to be answered in the form of an essay. There are no major differences between the General Training and Academic formats for task 2, except that the topics used in the questions may vary slightly, where themes such as *"Education"* or *"Environmental issues"* are more likely to appear in the Academic format, rather than *"TV"*, or *"Technology"* that may be more common in the General Training format.

There are three main question types in this part of the writing section:

a) Opposing-views question (Argument)

b) Opinion-based question (Proposal)

c) Two-part question (Discussion)

Suggested Answer Structure (Task 2)

The structure for the essay may vary somewhat according to the type of question provided, but generally speaking, the essay should be divided into four paragraphs.

	Essay Structure
Introduction	This paragraph should not be very long and it mainly consists of a brief paraphrase of the question. Important details to include are: - **The topic of the question** What is the essay about? Example: *"The use of mobile phones"* - **The outline of the essay or Thesis Statement** What aspects of the topic will be covered in the essay? Example: *"Advantages and disadvantages"*
First body paragraph	Each body paragraph will have the same structure: - **Topic sentence** The summary of the paragraph in one sentence Example: *"There are many advantages to using mobile phones for communication."* - **Explanation** What proves the topic sentence Example: *"One advantage is that using a cell phone allows people to communicate with others at anytime and anywhere."* - **Example(s)** What provides evidence for the explanation

	Example: *"For instance, if I get lost, I can contact my mother using my mobile in order to get instructions of how to get home from where I am."*
Second body paragraph	Same as above - **Topic sentence** - **Explanation** - **Example(s)**
Conclusion	A restatement of what the essay described or dealt with and a brief summary of the main points should be included. Example: *"To sum up, both pros and cons can be found when discussing the use mobile phones in terms of…"*

Scoring Criteria (Task 2)

Task 2 is assessed according to four areas which determine the final score in bands from 1 to 9. A brief description of each criterion is provided below:

Scoring Criteria Task 2	
Task response	This criterion assesses how well and thoroughly the question has been answered, as well as how much evidence is provided in the essay's development.
Cohesion and	This criterion assesses how well ideas are

Coherence	sequenced, connected, and organized. It also evaluates the use of Topic Sentences and paragraph structure.
Lexical resource	This criterion assesses the variety of vocabulary and level of sophistication and accuracy used.
Grammatical range and accuracy	This criterion assesses the variety of grammatical structures used and how well they are used in terms of the frequency of errors.

*The public version of the Writing scoring criteria is available on www.ielts.org

As it can be seen, there are no major variances between the scoring criteria for task 1 and 2. The main discrepancies are found in the first and second criteria, where the focus is on the content of the response and the structure used in Task 2.

Task 2 Question Types

Opposing-Views Question (formerly known as Argument)

Description

This question type refers to the cases where candidates are asked to analyse two sides of a topic/problem and present a personal opinion.

There are two cases in this question type:

Case 1) Advantage/disadvantage

In this case, a topic is given and the question asks to examine the advantages and disadvantages of it. An important aspect is that the development of the essay needs to impartial and the personal opinion should be stated at the end (conclusion) of the response.

Example:

> *Modern technology is being used more and more in different aspects of our lives, such as education. Do the **advantages** of using technology as an educational tool outweigh its **disadvantages**?*

Case 2) Some people say …/While others believe…

This case can be confusing because they will present two points of view or perspectives regarding the same topic. Most people think they are allowed to choose one side and describe that side only in their response, but contrary to that belief, candidates are requested to discuss both views (objectively) and then provide a personal position.

Example:

> ***Some people** believe that exams are essential to measure students' learning outcomes, **while others** believe that these assessments are unnecessary and unfair. What is your opinion?*

Opinion-Based Question (formerly known as Proposal)

This question type refers to the cases where candidates are asked to take a side regarding the statement presented in the question and provide their personal opinion about it. The difference between this question type and the former, is that in this case, candidates are free to choose the side they want to support, whereas in the *"opposing-views question type"*, both sides need to be analysed before an opinion is presented.

There are three cases in this question type:

Case 1) What is your opinion?

This case can seem rather ambiguous because the question itself is not very specific. A typical scenario is when a strong statement is provided and then an opinion is requested.

Example:

> More money should be spent on hiring and training the police force in order to reduce crime in big cities. What is **your opinion**?

Case 2) Do you agree or disagree?

This case is easy to identify because the question is always worded in the same way, by using the terms **agree** or **disagree**.

Example:

> Sports are the only way to keep youngsters out trouble and should be encouraged from an early age. Do you **agree** or **disagree** with this statement?

Case 3) To what extent do you agree or disagree?

This case is exactly the same as the previous one, but some people think that because the question is worded differently, they are being asked a different question. This is not the situation at all, it is just an alternative way to ask the same, which is the candidate's agreement towards the statement. The words used are: **To what extent** do you agree of disagree?

Example:

> *Children's leisure activities should always be educational because they have too much to learn before they become adults.* **To what extent** do you **agree** or **disagree**?

In other words, these three cases, reflect the same aim, which is to express agreement or disagreement in regards to the statement presented in the question.

A common misconception about these three cases is that some people believe the following:

- When the question is directly: ***do you agree or disagree?***, the only possible answer can either be full agreement or disagreement. This is not true.

- When the question states: ***to what extent do you agree or disagree?*** the only possible answer is to partly agree. Again, untrue.

The truth is, that regardless of the question received, if it belongs to the Opinion-based type, there are three possible answers:

I. Total agreement

II. Partial agreement

III. Total disagreement

In my experience, I can say that in most circumstances, a safer option is usually to partially agree. This is because choosing this option, would provide more arguments to include in the body paragraphs. When total agreement or disagreement are presented, the development tends to be quite narrow, and therefore weak.

Two-Part Question (formerly known as Discussion)

This question type refers to the cases in which candidates are given a problem or issue and are asked to discuss two questions/aspects about it. In other words, there are two parts to the question, hence the name.

There are two cases in this question type:

Case 1) Causes + Solutions or Effects

This case is easy to identify because the question is reasonably direct. It usually asks to explain the reasons that have produced a certain problem, and to provide suggestions/solutions or to discuss the effects this problem brings.

Example:

> In many countries there has been a noticeable increase of road accidents. What do you think are the **causes** of this? What **solutions** can you suggest?

Note that in this case, *"causes and effects"* or *"causes and solutions"* of a problem, there are two formats that can be used in the answer:

1) **Chain structure**: This is when one cause and one effect/solution are described in the same paragraph. The objective of this structure, is to present the ideas that are related. For example:

Causes and effects of pollution

> **Cause:** use of cars + **Solution:** people should use public transport more

2) **Block structure**: This structure is used when all the *causes* are described in one paragraph, and all the *effects/solutions* are dealt with in another paragraph. For example:

Causes and effects of pollution

> **Causes:**
> 1) use of cars
> 2) factory emissions
>
> **Solutions:**
> 1) people should be more eco-friendly
> 2) government should tax industries and car users

This structure is recommended when the *causes* and *effects/solutions* do not necessarily correlate each other. (*See samples provided below*)

Case 2) Question 1 + Question 2

This case can be more difficult to identify. The best way to recognize it is to count the number of questions being asked. The difference between this case and the former, is that in this instance, the questions are not necessarily related to each other. On the contrary, they are usually fairly independent from each other.

Example:

> *In some countries, the tenancy and use of fire arms is allowed for most people.* **Do you think** *that other countries should follow this trend?* **What problems** *could this bring?*

In summary, this question type requires candidates to discuss the two parts to the question in different body paragraphs. Each pat of the question should be dealt with independently.

Task 2 Question Types Summary

As explained above, there are mainly three question types in task 2. Many names have been given to these question categories, and the names do not really matter if the question is not answered correctly.

In my previous book, I called them: **Argument, Proposal** and **Discussion**. I have included those names in brackets () in this book, in order to help readers identify them better.

New names have been given this time, with the purpose making the categories more self-explanatory.

What this approach aims to do, is to provide a clear way to identify what questions request to do in order to maximize the score received in Task Response.

Therefore, three main categories have been described, each one proposing a different objective.

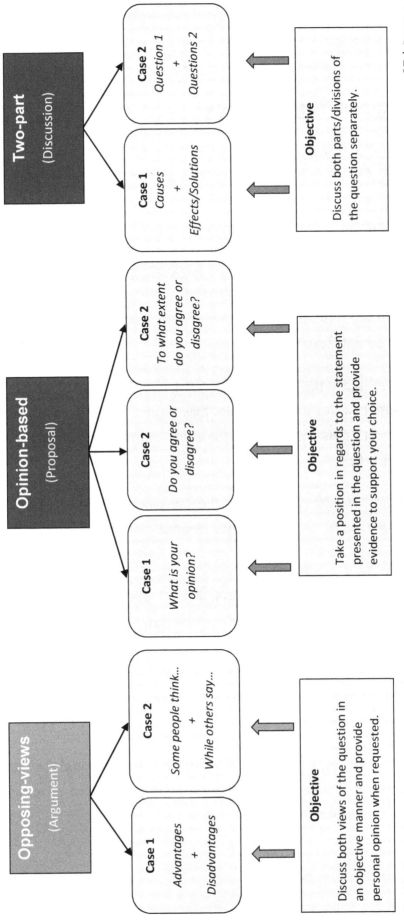

Planning Task 2 Essays

Planning essays is a step that most people try to avoid, because they think it is unnecessary and a waste of time. In my years helping people prepare for the IELTS, I have only encountered a small minority of students who understand how important planning is.

The biggest mistake is to think planning is optional. The reality is, that without a plan, people keep making the same mistakes over and over again which explains why some people hit a roof with their Writing score and cannot move forward.

I have had many students who come to me with a 6.5 in Writing and no matter how much they practice, they cannot seem to make any progress. In most cases their problem, is either the lack of planning, or planning incorrectly.

In other words, planning can be the difference between obtaining the desired score or not, so here is what needs to be understood about planning:

- **It is not a waste of time**. It is actually quite the contrary. Planning is an investment that in the long run, helps us save time. By having a clear plan of what we want to write, in the order we want to write it, with the examples we will use to support our ideas, we will save a big amount of time when we actually start writing and the process will be much smoother.

- **It is not, or at least it should not be, optional**. The main result that comes from not planning is having lack of unity, improvising and shifting in focus.

- **It should not take too long**, and it should be done in a key word system to avoid wasting time. Writing full sentences in a plan is definitely a waste of time, consequently, we should stick to concepts/key word that represent a whole patch of writing.

- **The more it is done, the faster/easier it becomes.** Like everything else in life, practice makes perfect.

Thus, it is vital to have a planning method to follow for task 2 that provides better results.

Steps to follow:

1) **Analize the question carefully**

    Too many people lose valuable points in Task Response due to not answering the question properly, which is usually a result of not studying the question carefully. When reading the question there are two factors to consider:

    a) *What type of question is it?*

    This is very important because by identifying the question type, the approach to use in the answer should be clear as well (objective, personal etc). This will increase the chances of getting a good score in Task Response.

    b) *What is the Topic of the question?*

    All questions have a common topic and sometimes sub-topics that need to be identified before starting the essay, otherwise the question will not be addressed fully.

This step should take between 2 to 3 minutes.

2) Chose what to plan for

Depending on how much practice a person has or how quickly someone can come up with ideas, there might be more or less to plan for. In general, a couple of ideas should be considered for the introduction, as well as the topic sentence for each body paragraph and the arguments and examples that will be provided in these paragraphs. Generally, planning for the conclusion is not necessary because this paragraph should be a summary of what has already been stated throughout the essay (see *Suggested answer structure* above). This step should take between 8 to 10 minutes.

What to plan for?

Introduction
What is the topic of the question?   What is the essay about?
First Body Paragraph
Topic Sentence   Argument 1 + Example   (Optional) Argument 2 + *Example*
Second Body Paragraph
Topic Sentence   Argument 1 + Example   (Optional) Argument 2 + *Example*

3) **Write the essay**

Once a good plan has been drafted, it is time to start writing. Ideally, this step should be as smooth and uninterrupted as possible to allow for flow. The more people stop while writing, the more disjointed ideas get. This step should take between 23 to 25 minutes to allow enough time for checking.

4) **Check and edit your essay**

And again, this should not be an optional *"if I have time" step*, but rather a compulsory part of the process that ensures a good end result. When editing, it is important to check if all ideas are clear, well-connected and organized. Most people just try to quickly fix their grammar errors but forget the other aspects being assessed. This step should take between 3 to 5 minutes.

Quick Tips For Task 2

1) Have a system and manage your time wisely.

There are a few external factors in the IELTS that we have absolute no control over. For instance, we cannot choose the question we will get, or the examiner that will mark our essay.

But there are some factors that we do have total control over, such as having a system. We can control how much we practice, what method to plan we use, how much we read in order to get ideas for our essays and how we manage our time.

Having a clear vision of how to tackle the writing, and in this case the essay, will help us boost our confidence and minimize the room for error.

2) Get familiar with the scoring criteria

It is nearly impossible not to be familiar with the scoring criteria and get good results. This is because examiners are trained to look for very specific features in IELTS essays.

So in order to tick all their boxes, we need to understand what their expectations are. In the previous chapter, we looked at the scoring criteria for task 1, which does not vary much from Task 2's.

The only criterion that is completely different is the first, which in this case is called Task response. Thus, in order to get a 7, the following needs to occur:

Task response

- Write at least 250 words and submit a finished essay

- Present clear position and provide enough evidence and support, though there may be a tendency to over-generalize.

- Cover all aspects of the question.

Cohesion and Coherence

- Present the information in a logical sequence where ideas progress at ease.

- Use a range of cohesive devices (linking words, pronoun reference etc) with some flexibility, though there may be some under/over-use

- Paragraphing should be adequate where there is good use of topic sentences.

Lexical range and accuracy

- Use a variety of expressions with some level of sophistication (uncommon words) and some awareness of style and collocation.

- Make a few errors throughout (most sentences are error-free) in terms of spelling, word choice and form.

Grammatical range and accuracy

- Have a variety of structures with a high level of accuracy (most sentences are error-free) and good control over punctuation.

As it can be seen, an essay that gets a 7 is far from being perfect, but it needs to have a high level of accuracy in all four criteria.

In order to get an 8, the requirements are the same but there is less scope for inaccuracy and higher expectations in terms of the proficiency and variety in the use of vocabulary and grammar.

3) Practice, practice and practice

The only way to improve in Writing is to practice so much, that it becomes mechanic or second nature. Each individual will have different strengths and weaknesses, but everybody needs to write as many times as possible in order to get better at it.

Reading is also important with the aim to be up-to-date with current affairs that might appear in the essay questions. Once difficulties have been identified, practice needs to be applied in those particular areas until the desired results are achieved.

For example, many of my students complain that it takes them too long to plan. Well, the response I give them is quite obvious, but sometimes the obvious is invisible to us.

I always say: *"Stop writing full essays. Take some time to write just plans. Time yourself. The first plan might take you 15 minutes to draft, the second hopefully 12 and the third maybe 10. It should only get better from there."*

Now that the essay structure, planning and question types have been explained, let us take a look at some model answers.

HIGH SCORING TASK 2 SAMPLE ANSWERS

Opposing-Views Question Type

Case 1 - Sample A

Write about the following topic:

Home-schooling has become very popular in recent years. However, most people still believe that attending schools is the best way to obtain a formal education. What are the advantages and disadvantages of home-schooling?

Give reasons for your answer and include any relevant examples from your own knowledge or experience.

Write at least 250 words.

Suggested Plan:

Topic: Home-schooling
Thesis Statement: Pros and Cons

Topic sentence: advantages of home-schooling
- **Advantage 1:** Tailor-made
- **Example:** children learn at their own pace
- **Advantage 2:** Safe environment
- **Example:** No bullying or risk of other dangers

Topic sentence: disadvantages of home-schooling
- **Disadvantage 1:** lack of socialization
- **Example:** children need interaction with peers
- **Disadvantage 2:** no extra-curricular activities
- **Example:** no opportunity to discover talents or skills

The way of parenting has radically changed over the last decade. Different styles have emerged and parents seem much more involved in their children's development. With this new model, many parents have decided to home-school their offspring instead of sending them to school. It is clear to see why this has become a popular new trend, but as in everything else, benefits and drawbacks need to be considered.

Firstly, some rather obvious advantages to home-schooling can be found. One of them, is the fact that the teaching method used either by parents or tutors can be modified to suit the child or children's needs. This means that children are able to learn at their own pace through the application of an approach that has been tailor-made considering their interests and learning styles. This is particularly valuable for children with disabilities or special needs. Additionally, a more secure environment can be provided for the child, where there are no dangers of being bullying or badly influenced by other pupils.

Contrarily, there are also negative aspects to this new trend. To start with, by studying at home children will miss out on a vital aspect of schools which is socialising with other children their age. Interacting with their peers is essential as it will help children develop all sorts of skills such as problem-solving, team work and leadership, all of which are important for the future professional life. Similarly, no matter how much effort parents put into making the home resemble the school environment, they will never be able to match the resources and extra-curricular activities that are available in schools, such as gyms, musical instruments or science laboratories. All of which would allow students to discover their talents and passions.

All in all, it is evident that home-schooling can be a beneficial experience for some children but given the limitations it involves, parents should consider all angles before deciding how to educate their children.

(343 words)

Case 1 - Sample B

Write about the following topic:

Modern technology is being used more and more in different aspects of our lives, such as education. Do the advantages of using technology as an educational tool outweigh its disadvantages?

Give reasons for your answer and include any relevant examples from your own knowledge or experience.

Write at least 250 words.

Suggested Plan:

Topic: Modern technology as educational tool
Thesis Statement: Outweigh Pros and Cons

Topic sentence: advantages of using tech as educational tool
- **Advantage 1:** dynamic
- **Example:** different resources: videos, apps, interactive books
- **Advantage 2:** we live in a high-tech world
- **Example:** everyone is exposed to tech devices, that is the future

Topic sentence: disadvantages of using tech as educational tool
- **Disadvantage 1:** can be distracting
- **Example:** counteractive effect
- **Disadvantage 2:** over-exposure to screen and tech
- **Example:** children are surrounded by screen and tech devices

We currently live in an era in which technology has become an essential part of our lives. These days, even schools have implemented technological resources in the classroom in order to aid teachers. Even though many people would agree that this is a positive practice, negative aspects should to be pondered as well.

Using technology as an educational instrument can definitely be a positive experience for students. First of all, it is undeniable that technology can bring dynamism to the classroom by incorporating an endless number of resources such as videos, applications pupils can use in their computers and even phones, interactive course books and so on, all of which are bound to capture students' attention. Additionally, it is a reality that our world will highly depend on technology in years to come. Which means that, introducing technology in schools may prepare children for their future, as they will certainly be exposed to these tools throughout their lives.

Nevertheless, on the down side of the matter, some drawbacks need to be taken into account. The first issue, is that technology can be quite distracting for students, especially younger ones, who may lack the discipline to focus on what the teacher is doing, and therefore, a counteractive effect can be seen. As a teacher myself, I struggle getting my students to concentrate in class when their phones are constantly beeping or vibrating. Another disadvantage, is that children are already overly exposed to screens, computers and other electric devices that can have a very detrimental effect on their development and can cause some health issues such as eye-sight problems, lack of sleep and even hyper-active behaviour.

In my opinion, it is clear to see that the application of technology in schools can be beneficial for students, but I think the disadvantages outweigh the benefits in terms of the negative effects that children would be exposed to.

(314 words)

Case 2 - Sample A

Write about the following topic:

Alcohol consumption has increased dramatically over the years. Some people believe that the government should increase taxes on alcoholic beverages but others oppose to this idea and advocate personal responsibility. What do you think?

Give reasons for your answer and include any relevant examples from your own knowledge or experience.

Write at least 250 words.

Suggested Plan:

Topic: increasing prices for alcoholic beverages
Thesis Statement: advocates and detractors

Topic sentence: reasons to support the price rise
- **Reason 1:** discourage consumption
- **Example:** higher prices might inhibit people from buying alcohol
- **Reason 2:** gov can use the taxes for positive policies
- **Example:** educating people about risks of excessive alcohol

Topic sentence: reasons to be against the measure
- **Reason 1:** free will
- **Example:** people should be able to choose what to do
- **Reason 2:** everyone pays the price
- **Example:** not all of us consume alcohol in big amounts

In today's society, the immoderate use of alcoholic beverages has alarmed governments around the world. This exorbitant consumption brings about all sorts of adverse effects such as street violence, over-dosing, especially among youngsters, and driving offenses. Given this scenario, some authorities have proposed increasing the levy on alcohol, which has divided the public's opinion into advocates and detractors.

It is clear to see why so many citizens would support this initiative. As a first point, this scheme would most likely discourage consumers from purchasing alcohol at a much higher price than they would otherwise pay for these products. Besides, the money collected from this additional tax can be spent on implementing projects that would benefit the entire community, such as educational programmes that aim to create awareness about the risks of uncontrolled use of alcohol, or building rehabilitation centres for those who have become addicted to this substance.

On the other hand, some rather convincing arguments can be found to oppose this policy. One of them, is the idea that the government would be interfering with people's free will by deciding what is better for them. Many people are against this view because they consider that each individual should be free to decide what they want to do with their lives, even if this brings harmful consequences. Also, some argue that by increasing the levy already imposed on alcohol, those who enjoy an occasional drink would pay the price for the reckless consumers, which can be considered an unfair outcome.

To sum up, I believe that ultimately, the government is responsible for protecting its citizens, and if a measure like this results in a decrease in the consumption of a beverage that tis known for altering people's behaviour, usually in a detrimental manner, then I support such intrusion.

(298 words)

Case 2 - Sample B

Write about the following topic:

Some people believe that dangerous criminals should spend the rest of their lives in prison, while others think that everyone deserves a second chance and that these offenders should be reintegrated into society. What is your opinion?

Give reasons for your answer and include any relevant examples from your own knowledge or experience.

Write at least 250 words.

Suggested Plan:

Topic: dangerous criminals
Thesis Statement: should get life sentence or be given another chance

---

Topic sentence: should spend life in prison
- **Reason 1:** community safety
- **Example:** protect innocent people
- **Reason 2:** repeat offenders
- **Example:** crime becomes a lifestyle

Topic sentence: should be part of society
- **Reason 1:** people can change
- **Example:** everyone makes mistakes
- **Reason 2:** prison can be worse in some cases
- **Example:** mistreatment

In a world where crime seems to gloomily be on the increase, what to do with inmates after they serve their sentence, has become a controversial issue. There are mainly two lines of thought, one that suggests that dangerous criminals should be kept in captivity for the rest of their lives, and those who believe that convicts should be reintegrated to society.

Understandably, those who support life sentence have strong motives to hold that opinion. A common argument, is the fact that law abiding citizens should not be put at risk by allowing minacious felons roam freely after they have served time in jail. It would be fair to say, that most people would react reluctantly towards a person they know has transgressed the law. Another point to consider, is the fact that many studies show that a high percentage of delinquents reoffend soon after they have been released, which would obviously concern many.

On the flip side of the coin, there are always groups of philanthropists that believe in second chances. These people believe that wrongdoing is part of human nature and that regardless of the severity of the crime, this should not define a person forever. Their thought is that everyone makes mistakes and therefore, we should kindly believe that people can change. Another reason to oppose keeping offenders in prison, is the fact that they might be subject to all kinds of abuse and they might even learn how to commit more crimes if they are ever released. As some say, there is no better school than prison.

In my perspective, it is difficult to choose a side in regards to this issue. I think that each case should be treated independently and enough filters should be put in place to make sure that criminals who are freed do not reoffend.

(304 words)

Opinion-based Question Type

Case 1 - Sample A

Write about the following topic:

Traffic congestion is a serious problem in most big cities. Some people believe that governments should build more roads. What do you think about this solution?

Give reasons for your answer and include any relevant examples from your own knowledge or experience.

Write at least 250 words.

Suggested Plan:

Topic: traffic congestion
Thesis Statement: building new roads is a good solution with a huge obstacle

Topic sentence: good solution
- **Reason 1:** ease congestion
- **Example:** Melbourne
- **Reason 2:** better connectivity
- **Example:** Melbourne

Topic sentence: impact on residents
- **Reason 1:** land acquisition
- **Example:** my grandparents

Most big cities suffer from the increasing problem of excessive traffic. Dwellers in mega metropolises such as Moscow, put up with hours of driving short distances. Some people have suggested that a way to tackle this issue is to construct more roads. I tend to think this is a good solution, although there is an important aspect to consider.

To begin with, this measure would be positive for two main reasons. The first point, is that having additional roads, especially highways, would greatly ease traffic congestion as cars, trucks and buses would be spread out in different areas. Another reason, is that new paths would also allow for better connectivity between suburbs. An illustration of these points is Melbourne, where population has grown substantially over the last few decades and as a result, the use of private cars has picked as well. The provision of new freeways that connect the southern, northern, eastern and western suburbs, allow people to efficiently travel the long distances of this big city.

As an opposite perspective, it is also important to consider the residents who would be severely affected by this developments. As a first argument, in order to build more roads, land acquisition would most likely take place. This means that residents living in the prospective are of construction, lose their properties, and though get compensated for it, would have no choice but to relocate. I witnessed this first hand when my grandparents' house was acquired by the government because it was situated in an area where a new train station was projected. Even though they got remunerated for their property, my grandparents had to leave the house where they raised their children, had a life and planned on staying for the rest of their lives.

All angles considered, I believe that progress sometimes has a high price tag that only a handful pay. For this reason, I think that the need for building new roads has to be justified enough to make it worth it for those who would have leave their homes for the greater good.

(345 words)

Case 1- Sample B

Write about the following topic:

More money should be spent on hiring and training the police force in order to reduce crime in big cities. What is your opinion?

Give reasons for your answer and include any relevant examples from your own knowledge or experience.

Write at least 250 words.

Suggested Plan:

Topic: more training for police force to reduce crime
Thesis Statement: partly agree

Topic sentence: good solution
- **Reason 1:** better to prevent crime

Topic sentence: crime is complex
- **Reason 1:** roots of crime
- **Example:** USA

How to reduce crime is a wildly discussed topic by most authorities, especially around election time. The fact of the matter is that crime has intensified worldwide. Some say that having more and better trained police officers might help reduce delinquency. However, I believe that while this might be the case, the depth of the problem needs to be examined as well.

On one hand, I do think this solution may contribute positively. Clearly, prevention is always a preferred method in any situation. This means that higher numbers of officers on the streets could potentially discourage criminals to break the law, knowing that there is more surveillance and consequently they may run a higher risk of getting caught. Additionally, improved preparation for the police force would better-equip them to foresee criminal activity and stop it before it occurs. For instance, top of the range technology and special training has allowed the stoppage of potential terrorist attacks in Australia.

On the other hand, crime is a very complex issue that requires further consideration. The roots of crime are so varied and intricate that it is hard to imagine that, only having more policemen, would solve the problem. These days the motivations criminals have to act are quite often unpredictable. The lack of social protection and support for vulnerable people is what often leads to illegal activity. A good example of this is the US where millions are invested in the creation of new prisons, but nothing has been done in regard to gun possession even though this is one of the countries with the highest number of mass shootings, which kills and injures hundreds each year.

In sum, I believe that more resources should be spent not only on training and hiring police officers but also providing better welfare for citizens around the world, which in my opinion would be the most efficient method to avert illegal activity.

(317 words)

Case 2- Sample A

Write about the following topic:

It is currently believed that children's behaviour and misconduct is due to the lack of strict discipline and punishment applied by parents. Do you agree or disagree with this statement?

Give reasons for your answer and include any relevant examples from your own knowledge or experience.

Write at least 250 words.

Suggested Plan:

Topic: children's behaviour caused by parent's leniency
Thesis Statement: partly agree

Topic sentence: Agree
- **Reason 1:** parenting models have changed
- **Example:** tantrums at shops

Topic sentence: Disagree
- **Reason 1:** other factors
- **Example:** external influence

It is common to hear experts' concern about the younger generation and their poor behaviour. Some believe that the main cause of this tendency is the lack of discipline applied by parents. Although I believe this is true to certain degree, I also think there are other factors to be considered.

First of all, I believe this this phenomenon has been aggravated by the endless array of information available for parents. New models of parenting have arisen and with these, a sometimes misleading number of strategies on how to parent have become widely accepted. Advice on what to do with children from when they are born to when they become adults is accessible in books, blogs and even hospitals. Practices previous generations applied such as grounding children or using the word "no" to teach them they cannot always get what they want, are now regarded as old-fashioned and even cruel. A good illustration of this is a visit to any shop, where a common scene is to find a crying child and a mortified mother or father who vainly tries to discipline his or her child, but ends up giving in to the child's whim to stop the crying and the strangers' pity looks.

Conversely, some would argue that parents are not the only factor. This is because it is undeniable that regardless of the parents' efforts, children nowadays have access to an assortment of information from a variety of media channels that no other previous generation has experienced before. This would clearly have an impact on the youngsters' behaviour. Additionally, friends are usually one of the biggest influences in a person's life. Therefore, the type of friends our children have would absolutely have an effect on how they act and how they treat others. We have all most likely been victims of peer pressure, and I would say at least from experience, it is nothing to be proud of.

To conclude, I do believe that parents are the primary source of guidance for children. But I also believe that regardless of how hard parents try to teach their children good manners and conduct, there will always be other sources of influence in their lives out of the parents' control.

(370 words)

Case 2- Sample B

Write about the following topic:

Children's leisure activities should always be educational because they have too much to learn before they become adults. Do you agree or disagree?

Give reasons for your answer and include any relevant examples from your own knowledge or experience.

Write at least 250 words.

Suggested Plan:

Topic: children's free time should be educational
Thesis Statement: disagree

Topic sentence: childhood is too short
- **Reason 1:** children need playtime for development
- **Example:** only a quarter of a person's life

Topic sentence: too much emphasis in academic learning
- **Reason 1:** inhibits creativity
- **Example:** children need to find their skills and abilities

In the busy and competitive world we live in, it is common to see parents worry about their children's education much more than in the past. Some say, that all activities infants take part in should have an educational focus in order for them to learn as much as possible before becoming adults. Personally, I tend to disagree with this statement.

To begin with, childhood is one of the shortest stages of a person's life. Many experts have confirmed that children require several hours of pure playtime in order to develop their minds and bodies comprehensively. From the moment they are born, children are ready to explore the world. They will have plenty of time in their future lives to learn the theory of how everything works and be given all sorts of responsibilities. With the expanding life expectancy, almost reaching a hundred these days, it is fair to say that childhood only accounts for about a quarter of a person's life, and this time should be spent discovering the world around them rather than focusing on just learning.

Additionally, I believe far too much emphasis is placed on academic learning. Currently, most countries impose long school regimes in which children must be in class for an average of seven hours a day. After school, they need to attend other chores which usually include more work such as school assignments and projects. This in turn, can inhibit creativity as children are left with virtually no time to discover their talents and abilities which is essential for their happiness. It seems as though governments have lost sight of what the educational system should be about and is creating the concept that Mathematics and Science are more important than Art and Music.

In a nutshell, it is my belief that children should be given more time to be free and do activities they are truly interested in, which will help them discover what they are passionate about. Our job as a society should be to form happy children as opposed to impose learning experiences all the time.

(345 words)

Case 3- Sample A

Write about the following topic:

Sports events such as the Formula One and other car racing events should be banned because they are an unnecessary waste of money and create more pollution. To what extent do you agree or disagree with this statement?

Give reasons for your answer and include any relevant examples from your own knowledge or experience.

Write at least 250 words.

Suggested Plan:

Topic: Banning of sporting events like F1 due to waste of money and pollution
Thesis Statement: Disagree but changes should be made

Topic sentence: Disagree
- **Reason 1:** Many people love Formula 1
- **Example:** Buzz, energy and excitement

Topic sentence: Take more responsibility
- **Reason 1:** Food & drink waste
- **Example:** Give left-overs to homeless

Sporting events, such as Formula 1, are incredibly popular across the world and generate enormous interest from fans and the media. However, Formula 1 is known to waste significant sums of money and also create additional pollution than we already have, which is why some say it should be banned. In my opinion, these events should not be prohibited but people behind these sports should take more responsibility for the negative effects these activities have on society and the environment.

Firstly, one argument to oppose this measure is that it would leave numerous people without a passion. Having been to several Formula 1 events, it is not difficult to see the enjoyment that so many people get from following and attending each Formula 1 race. People travel from all over the world to visit races, which not only generates revenue for the local economy, but also brings world attention to each race location. I myself love the exhilaration and energy of the event and love watching the excitement and intensity of the race. I will certainly bring my children to races in the future because it is a really enjoyable day out.

However, this is not to say that the Formula 1 governing body should not take more responsibility for the negative effects it has. The statistics of food and drinks that are provided for each race is incredibly high, but so is the amount of it that goes to waste. For example, it would be a responsible idea for the Formula 1 governing body to give any left-over food to homeless shelters or organisations that help disadvantaged people. In addition, modifying the car engines in order to lower the levels of pollution that the cars emit would also show that they are taking responsibility for the environment.

In summary, even though events like the Formula 1 do have some negative effects, the enjoyment and passion it provides to people all over the world significantly outweighs the negatives. However, anything that the governing body can do to be more accountable for the negative effects, is certainly something that they should be strongly aim to do.

(355 Words)

Case 3- Sample A

Write about the following topic:

Animal testing has always been a controversial issue. Some people believe that governments should ban these practices completely. To what extent do you agree or disagree with this statement?

Give reasons for your answer and include any relevant examples from your own knowledge or experience.

Write at least 250 words.

Suggested Plan:

Topic: The banning of animal testing
Thesis Statement: Partly agree

Topic sentence: Agree
- **Reason 1:** Animals have feelings
- **Example:** rabbits

Topic sentence: Disagree
- **Reason 1:** positive research
- **Example:** immunizations

Testing on animals is a practice that has been conducted for many years and for a variety of reasons. Some people strongly disagree with animal testing and believe that governments should discontinue it altogether. In my opinion, it would be preferable not to test on animals, but there are many reasons to be grateful for the results of this practice.

To begin with, animals that are used for testing all have feelings of pain and discomfort. Many of us choose not to know what actually happens in laboratories where these experiments take place, because it is obvious that this would not be an enjoyable sight. Clearly, the primary reason to experiment on animals is to analyse the way they react to certain substances in order to conclude whether these would be safe for humans. Consequently, it is only expectable that animals that are tested on would experience a huge amount of stress, pain and anxiety. For instance, it is known that certain shampoo brands use rabbits to test their products to see if any kind of skin reaction appears. Needless to say, this must be quite a painful procedure for the animals that get skin rashes as a result of the experiment.

However, it cannot be denied that great discoveries have been made through animal testing. Diseases that used to be lethal have now been nearly eradicated thanks to medical research, which has made it possible for us to have medicine that can prevent the spread of such illnesses. A good illustration of this is immunizations, which are now available to most people, in most countries, to be used from the birth, preventing a considerable number of deaths by contracting ailments such tuberculosis or the whooping cough. Unfortunately, none of these advancements would be possible without testing on animals.

To conclude, animal testing is a controversial issue simply because it is a practice that is not completely moral. But I have to advocate for the benefits that this practice has brought to the health and safety of humankind.

(338 Words)

Two-part Question Type

Case 1 - Sample A

Write about the following topic:

The use of recreational drugs is on the increase, especially among young people. Describe the reasons for this worrying issue and provide suggestions to minimize it.

Give reasons for your answer and include any relevant examples from your own knowledge or experience.

Write at least 250 words.

Suggested Plan:

Topic: Use of recreational drugs among young people
Thesis Statement: causes and solutions

- **Topic sentence:** Access of drugs
  - **Cause:** Drugs dealers make it easy to get
  - **Suggestion:** Check people more thoroughly

- **Topic sentence:** unhappiness
  - **Cause:** emotional pain
  - **Suggestion:** Provide more support

Recreational drugs are an ever increasing habit for many young people across the world. Not only is this very concerning for society in general, but the effects this has on young people can be debilitating for their future lives. There are two key reasons for this worrying issue, but some measures can help mitigate the problem.

Firstly, a major reason for this increase is how disturbingly easy it is to either buy or get access to drugs these days. Not only are there dealers constantly making themselves available to young people, but the ever growing supply makes drugs cheap as well. For instance, it is known that in most popular parties or night clubs, people can buy practically any drug they wish even when these places are controlled by security. An effective solution for these common situations would be to improve the level of security in such events by increasing the number of guards, thoroughly checking attendees' belongings and denying access to any suspicious people. This measure would considerably decrease the availability, and thus, consumption of illegal substances.

In addition, the current volumes of drug consumption can be attributed to the high levels of dissatisfaction many people experience these days. The dissolution of the family unit, constant and imminent wars, heart break and death are many triggers that make some people want to escape their pain and use substances that will allow them to evade these feelings, even if just for a while. In order to rectify this predicament, families should be more observant of their loved ones and be wary of any changes in behaviour and offer their unconditional support. Likewise, authorities should put more systems in place, which can aid vulnerable people to access help in situations when they may be isolated from their families, such as homeless youngsters, ex-soldiers and unemployed people.

In summary, recreational drugs are certainly having an immense impact on young people because of the increase in use. However, there are several measures that can be taken to minimize and limit the use. Implementing stricter security where drugs are easily available and providing more support will go a long way to helping this issue.

(360 Words, chain structure used)

Case 1 - Sample B

Write about the following topic:

An increasing number of couples have adopted a 'childless' lifestyle over the last decades. What do you think is causing this? What effects will this trend have on society?

Give reasons for your answer and include any relevant examples from your own knowledge or experience.

Write at least 250 words.

Suggested Plan:

Topic: Couples with no children
Thesis Statement: Causes and effects on society

Topic sentence: Causes
- **Reason 1:** busy lifestyle
- **Example:** career focus
- **Reason 2:** no responsibility
- **Example:** more free time

Topic sentence: Positive and negative Effects
- **Reason 1:** Positive, more tax for gov
- **Example:** Australia
- **Reason 2:** Negative, older population

New ways of having a family have come to be more accepted and the old roles of men and women seem to be part of the past. Together with these changes, a new movement of couples who decide not to have children has become more common, introducing a child-free lifestyle. Some of the causes and effects of this trend will be analysed as follows.

Firstly, different reasons can be found when it comes to this trend. To start with, a major cause would be the modern and busy way of living. Life has become much more demanding than 20 years ago. These days, people need to not only have one degree, but ideally pursue a post-degree in order to compete in today's market. For this reason, some couples are too occupied building their careers to consider having progeny. Additionally, many couples prefer to have a more flexible way of life that allows them to travel or partake in activities which children may difficult. I personally have several friends and even family members who have chosen not to have children because they say they are too busy enjoying life without the responsibility it involves to be a parent.

Consequently, this life choice may bring positive and negative effects to society. Governments that provide free welfare with tax-payers' money would benefit from this drift. This is because there would be fewer people in need of social aid, such as childcare allowances. An illustration of this is Australia, where people who have children receive a series of social help such as a baby bonus and all kinds of rebates. However, an inevitable negative impact would be a rising aging population, which would affect the economy of the country in several ways. More stress would be placed on age-care and there would be a higher demand for skilled professionals in any new career paths. An example of this is Japan, where population has decreased by the lowering birth rates.

All in all, it is clear to see why so many people are choosing to have a child-free lifestyle and it is expectable that this trend increase over the next few years. But the consequences need to be addressed in order to prevent social problems in the future.

(373 words)

Case 2 - Sample A

Write about the following topic:

Advertising is the most commonly used tool for companies to sell their products. In what aspects of our life is advertising present? What effects can advertising have on people?

Give reasons for your answer and include any relevant examples from your own knowledge or experience.

Write at least 250 words.

Suggested Plan:

Topic: advertising
Thesis Statement: where is it, what effects does it have on people?

Topic sentence: presence of advertisement
- **Reason 1:** everywhere
- **Example:** internet, TV, roads

Topic sentence: effects on people
- **Effect 1:** Positive, inform customers
- **Example:** sales, special features
- **Effect 2:** Negative, misleading
- **Example:** food

Advertising surrounds virtually everybody in the entire world every day. In fact, we get consumed by advertising without us consciously knowing about it. However, there are specific aspects of our lives in which advertising is more present. Furthermore, there are also certain effects that this can have on people.

To begin with, advertising is very present in every aspect of our lives. Wherever we go or look, we are bombarded by propaganda. Whether we like it or not, advertising is not a choice anymore but compulsory viewing. Companies know that the more presence they have, the more people will feel the need to use their products. For this reason, they have taken possession of every media available to publicize their brand. Examples of this can be found in all kinds of activities we do daily, for instance, doing an internet search will prompt all sorts of commercials on both sides of a webpage and even pop-up windows. When driving, it is possible to notice billboards and banners. Finally, television and radio would not be possible without the support of sponsors who pay channels and stations for promotion.

Nonetheless, the effects of this constant propaganda exposure should not be overlooked. Firstly, it can be beneficial to have access to advertisement. People can get informed about special sales or specific features of different products which can help customers take advantage of these opportunities or get better-informed about a good. On the other hand, it is undeniable that advertising can be quite misleading. Sometimes companies use their media exposure to promote certain products which can be said to have qualities when in reality it may be the opposite case. A good example of this is food, where the products that are publicized the most, tend to be the unhealthiest, such as junk food, or sugary drinks.

In conclusion, it can be affirmed that we are surrounded by advertising wherever we go and the impacts of this constant propaganda exposure can be positive or negative for customers.

(333 words)

Case 2 - Sample B

Write about the following topic:

More and more women have joined the work force in recent years. What reasons do women have to be more professionally driven? What effects does this trend have on their families?

Give reasons for your answer and include any relevant examples from your own knowledge or experience.

Write at least 250 words.

Suggested Plan:

Topic: More women participation in workforce
Thesis Statement: reasons and effects

Topic sentence: why women work more
- **Reason 1:** women's new role in society
- **Example:** politics and business
- **Reason 2:** family needs
- **Example:** cost of life

Topic sentence: effects on society
- **Effect 1:** Positive, more diversity
- **Example:** men and women complement each other
- **Effect 2:** Negative, less quality time with children

All around the world, we have seen a shift in the participation of women in society. What used to be unthinkable has now become the norm, for instance, the US is about to have the first female president. These days women are more career focused than their counterparts 20 years ago. I believe there are various reasons for these changes and inevitably, there will be consequences for society as well.

First of all, it is important to analyse what has caused this movement. One reason women have become more professionally active is the role of women, which has radically changed. Women used to be the carers of the family, responsible for the nourishment and education of children and house chores. Nowadays, more and more women have access to education, which atomically leads to a desire to develop a professional career. Another aspect, is the fact that most households need a double income to support their families. The cost of life has risen considerably in most countries, which has made it almost compulsory for women to have to become professionally active.

From another angle, the effects of these changes can also vary. On the positive side, it can be said that the participation of women in the workforce makes the working environment much more diverse and integral. Female workers have as much or more expertise and knowledge to share and contribute with, and they are the perfect complement for their male counterpart, which may assure a more equitable dynamic work space. Nevertheless, some might worry that having women work more, may bring adverse effects such as the disintegration of the family in extreme cases, or the negligence of children who may be left alone for long periods of time while both parents work.

To sum up, it is clear to see that the increase of female involvement in the work force has been caused mainly by social changes. These can bring both positive and negative effects to society.

(327 words)

ABOUT THE AUTHOR

Daniella Moyla

Daniella is a highly sought after IELTS consultant due to her ability to make IELTS easy for people to understand.

Daniella is a degree qualified English teacher with expertise in ESL, academic English, TOEFL and IELTS preparation.

Born in Chile, English is not her first language which has allowed her to understand the difficulties faced by anyone taking the IELTS exam.

Daniella has written several IELTS training courses which demonstrates her comprehensive understanding of the IELTS and the requirements for achieving a high score.

Her love of teaching also inspires her to continue following her passion of helping as many people as possible pass the IELTS.

CPSIA information can be obtained
at www.ICGtesting.com
Printed in the USA
LVHW102310230821
695911LV00011B/1134